THE ELEMENTS

Chromium

Nathan Lepora

mc **Marshall Cavendish**
Benchmark
New York

Marshall Cavendish Benchmark
99 White Plains Road
Tarrytown, New York 10591

www.marshallcavendish.us

Library of Congress Cataloging-in-Publication Data

Lepora, Nathan.
Chromium / Nathan Lepora.
    p.   cm. — (The elements)
         Includes index.

ISBN-13 978-0-7614-1920-4
ISBN 0-7614-1920-9
1. Chromium—Juvenile literature. I. Title. II. Elements (Marshall
Cavendish Benchmark)
QD181.C7L47 2005
546'.532—dc22

2005042160

6 5 4 3 2

Printed in China

Picture credits
Front cover: Photos.com
Back cover: Photos.com

Stan Celestian: 10
Corbis: Lester Lefkowitz 20, Danny Lehman 23
Getty Images: Luis Velga 6
Hemera: 26
Outokumpu Oyj: 11, 13
Photos.com: 7, 25
Science Photo Library: Andrew Lambert Photography 30, Martyn F Chillmaid 24,
Arnold Fisher 1, 8, Coneyl Jay 27, Jesse 21, Russ Lappa 4, Richard Megna/Fundamental Photos 19,
David Taylor 17, Charles D Winters 3, 12, 16
University of Pennsylvania Library: Edgar Fahs Smith Collection 9

Series created by The Brown Reference Group plc.
Designed by Sarah Williams
www.brownreference.com

Contents

What is chromium?

Chromium is a silver-gray metal that has a beautiful shine when polished. It is commonly seen as reflective "chrome" coatings on items like car bumpers, and the metal is an ingredient in stainless steel. People also need tiny amounts in their food to help control the amount of sugar in their blood.

Like most other metals, chromium combines with other elements to form compounds. Chromium compounds are usually brightly colored.

They give ruby and emerald gemstones their color and are used in paints and dyes. The most common natural form of chromium is a striking orange mineral called chromite.

The chromium atom

There are more than ninety elements in nature. All matter is made from the elements—either pure, in mixtures, or as chemical compounds. Chromium is one of the elements. In normal conditions, it is a hard, metallic solid.

Pure chromium is a hard silvery metal. It is rarely found in a pure state in nature. Chromium metal has to be extracted from ore.

Everything on Earth is made from atoms. One pound (0.45 kg) of any material contains more than a million billion billion of these tiny units. Solid elements, such as chromium, have their atoms arranged in repeating stacks.

Atoms are made from even smaller particles. At the center of an atom is a nucleus. Tiny particles called electrons circle the nucleus. Each electron has a negative electric charge. The nucleus is positively charged. Because opposite charges attract each other, the negative electrons stay close to the positively charged nucleus.

Atomic number and mass

Inside an atom's nucleus are particles called protons and neutrons. These have about the same mass and size as each other. A proton carries a positive electric charge, while the neutron is neutral and does not have an electric charge. These particles are clumped together to make the dense nucleus.

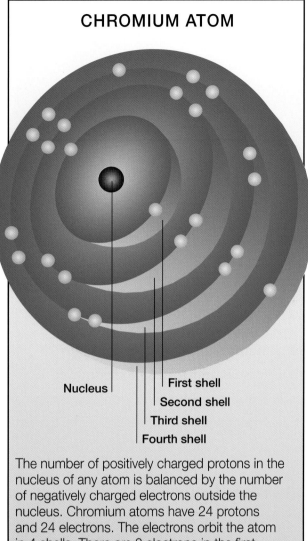

CHROMIUM ATOM

Nucleus | First shell
Second shell
Third shell
Fourth shell

The number of positively charged protons in the nucleus of any atom is balanced by the number of negatively charged electrons outside the nucleus. Chromium atoms have 24 protons and 24 electrons. The electrons orbit the atom in 4 shells. There are 2 electrons in the first shell, 8 in the second, 13 in the third, and 1 in the fourth shell.

DID YOU KNOW?

ORIGIN OF THE NAME
Chromium was named for the ancient Greek word *chromos*, which means "color." The French chemist Louis-Nicolas Vauquelin (1763–1829) named the metal in 1797 after discovering it in a bright orange mineral called crocoite. The name chromium was well chosen because many other chromium compounds are vividly colored.

Scientists describe an atom with two numbers. The atomic mass number includes the protons plus the neutrons. The atomic number tells the number of protons in the atom. Each element has a unique atomic number. The atomic number of chromium is 24. Chromium atoms usually contain 28 neutrons to make an atomic

mass number of 52 (24 protons plus 28 neutrons). Rarer forms of chromium—called isotopes—have 29 or 30 neutrons. These isotopes have a higher atomic mass number than most chromium atoms.

Electron shells

All atoms have no overall charge. For atoms to have no charge, the numbers of electrons and protons must be the same. A chromium atom contains twenty-four protons and twenty-four electrons.

Atoms of different elements bond together into structures called molecules. When elements form molecules, they take part in chemical reactions. Chemical reactions occur when atoms share electrons.

Each shell around the nucleus of an atom can only hold a certain number of electrons. Shells are considered full when

Emerald gemstones get their green color from a very small number of chromium atoms in the crystals. Without the chromium the crystals would be clear.

they have the most electrons possible. An atom's inner shells are usually full. But the outer shell usually lacks a certain number of electrons. An element's chemistry is determined by how many electrons its outer shell is missing. Mostly only the outer shell is involved in moving electrons.

Of a chromium atom's four shells, the inner two shells are full. But the third shell contains thirteen of a possible eighteen electrons. The outer shell has one electron out of a full set of eight. This makes chromium's chemistry more complex than other elements because chromium atoms can lose or gain electrons from both the third and outer shells.

Special characteristics

Chromium is used to make a shiny "chrome" covering that protects other metals from corrosion.

Chemists arrange the elements in a periodic table according to their atomic mass numbers. Chromium is the twenty-fourth element and sits in a section of the table known as the transition metals. These metals typically use electrons in their two outermost shells for chemical reactions. This means that chromium, like other transition metals, has a special chemistry. It can form many different combinations with the same elements.

Chromium lies close to iron in the periodic table. Because of this, these two elements share many chemical and physical properties. Both are hard metals with high melting and boiling points. They also conduct heat and electricity well.

Pure chromium does not chemically react with many substances. This makes it resistant to corrosion. (Corrosion is when objects react with air and become weaker.) Chromium is used to protect other metals from corrosion. For example, it is used to coat iron objects to stop them from rusting.

CHROMIUM FACTS	
⬤ Chemical symbol:	Cr
⬤ Atomic number:	24
⬤ Atomic mass:	52
⬤ Melting point:	3375 °F (1907 °C)
⬤ Boiling point:	4842 °F (2671 °C)
⬤ Density:	7.14 grams in every cubic cm. (7.14 times denser than water.)

History of chromium

Unlike more common metals such as iron and copper, chromium has only been known by scientists for two hundred years. After its discovery in the late eighteenth century, brightly colored chromium compounds became popular in paints and clothing dyes. In the early twentieth century chromium began to be used in stainless steel.

Chromium's discovery

Chromium was first discovered in a mineral called crocoite. (A mineral is a naturally occurring compound.) The German prospector Johann Gottlieb Lehmann (1719–1767) first wrote about this red-orange mineral in 1761, calling it red lead. He analyzed samples from a Siberian mine and wrongly thought they were made from the heavy metals lead and selenium.

It was not until the French chemist Nicolas-Louis Vauquelin received some crystals of crocoite in 1797 that scientists realized the importance of the mineral. Vauquelin's studies showed the crystals contained lead and a completely new metallic element.

Crocoite often forms needle-like crystals. The mineral is also called lead chromate.

DISCOVERERS

NICOLAS-LOUIS VAUQUELIN

Nicolas-Louis Vauquelin was a hard-working French chemist. He published 378 scientific papers that mainly describe how to isolate chemicals. Vauquelin is credited with discovering chromium in 1797, but his work also helped to discover another element called beryllium. Vauquelin was the first to make a compound containing beryllium, which he did using a type of gemstone called beryl in 1798. However, pure beryllium metal was isolated only thirty years later. Vauquelin was also the first person to study amino acids (the building blocks of protein). He extracted them from asparagus plants.

Nicolas-Louis Vauquelin was the first person to make pure chromium metal.

When Vauquelin first found chromium, he only extracted chromium oxide (CrO_3). This is a compound of chromium and oxygen. In 1798 he obtained the pure metal. He also found traces of chromium in ruby and emerald gemstones. Vauquelin correctly guessed that chromium gives the stones their colors.

Industrial uses

In the early nineteenth century, people used chromium compounds mainly for coloring paints and clothes dyes.

A particularly popular color was chromium yellow, or lead chromate ($PbCrO_4$). This is a humanmade version of crocoite. Soon, other chromium-containing chemicals were being used for processes such as tanning leather.

The large-scale use of chromium began in the 1900s after the invention of the electric arc furnace. This machine could refine large amounts of ore into a mixture, or alloy, of iron and chromium. This alloy has been widely used ever since as stainless steel. By 1798 people found a way to isolate pure chromium. Chromium became a popular protective shiny "chrome" coating for metals objects, such as cutlery.

Where chromium is found

Chromium almost never occurs as a pure metal in nature. Instead, it is found combined with other elements such as iron, lead, and oxygen in natural compounds called minerals and ores.

Scientists estimate that the Earth's crust contains about 0.01 percent chromium. This makes chromium less common than iron but more abundant than rare metals like gold. Although most chromium ore is buried deep underground, scientists believe there is a plentiful supply for the future.

Ores

An ore is a rock or mineral that contains a source of metal. (Minerals are crystals made from a single compound, while rocks are combinations of different minerals.) The main ore of chromium is the mineral chromite. This chemical is a

This rock contains a lot of chromite ore. Chromite is an oxide of chromium and iron. Chromite is refined into a mixture of pure chromium and iron atoms.

compound of iron, chromium, and oxygen ($FeCr_2O_4$). Many countries mine chromite. South Africa, Kazakhstan, and India produce the most.

One of the few places where chromium is found as a naturally pure metal is in the Udachna diamond mine in Russia. The conditions that made the diamonds also formed pure chromium.

Chromium's origin

Chromium has existed on Earth since the planet was formed about 4.5 billion years ago. The metal was contained in asteroids

The Kemi mine in Finland digs out 2 million tons (1.8 million tonnes) of chromite every year.

DID YOU KNOW?

TYPES OF ROCK

Geologists classify rocks into three different types. Igneous rocks come from hot liquid rock. This hot liquid rose from inside Earth and either erupted from volcanoes or cooled on the underside of Earth's crust. Sedimentary rocks are made from sediments that settled at the bottom of the ocean. Examples include chalk and limestone, which are made from the shells of ancient sea animals. Metamorphic rocks are igneous or sedimentary rocks that have been squashed or heated in earthquakes or under mountains. All chromium ores are igneous rocks.

that smashed into each other to make the planet. The early planet was as a ball of hot liquid. Heavy substances, like most metals including chromium, sank into the center of the growing planet. Lighter compounds floated on the surface and eventually cooled to make the planet's rocky crust. Chromium and other metals are still most common in Earth's liquid center.

Sometimes, the hot liquids from deep inside Earth ooze up through cracks in the seafloor. This creates a layer of chromium minerals, along with other rocks. Over millions of years, movements in Earth's crust push these rocks up from the seafloor to make dry land. These rock layers are the chromium ores mined today.

11

Mining and refining

Chromium is an important metal for industry. More than $2 billion worth of chromium is produced every year. About 14 million tons (12.7 million tonnes) of chromium ore are refined to produce 5 million tons (4.5 million tonnes) of chromium. Of this, 3.5 million tons (3 million tonnes) are sold as a mixture of iron and chromium called ferrochromium.

Mining

Mining chromium ore is similar to digging up other ores. If the ore is near the Earth's surface then it is dug out of a huge hole called an open pit. The ore is blasted out of the ground with explosives and taken away on conveyer belts or gigantic trucks. Ore buried deeper below ground is dug out of an underground mine. Miners dig tunnels down to the ore. Then the ore is blasted out and removed in containers.

Deposits of chromium ore have two main shapes, which depend on how the ore was formed after erupting in a hot liquid. The most common shape is a thin layer. These deposits are called stratiform deposits. (The geological word *strata* refers to a layer of rock.) In a few places the ore is not layered but scattered in blobs. These are caused when the chromium ore spreads through hot liquid rock underground.

Although most refineries produce chromium mixed with iron, some make pure chromium by reacting it with aluminum. This reaction produces a lot of heat and light.

Refining

Huge industrial complexes called refineries extract the chromium from the ore through a variety of chemical processes. A typical refinery covers several acres and consumes enough electricity to power a small town. Refineries are often built very close to the mine to lower the cost of transporting the ore.

The purpose of refining is to separate the chromium atoms from the other elements in the compound. Most chromium refineries do this by smelting. In this process the ore is mixed with fuel in a large furnace, or smelter. The furnace burns coke fuel, which is pure carbon made by roasting coal. The furnace may also be heated using electricity. The coke reacts with the ore to remove unwanted elements, which form waste called slag. In the hot mixture, the liquid chromium sinks to the bottom. It is then separated off leaving the slag behind.

Ferrochromium

Chromite is a compound of iron, chromium, and oxygen. Refining chromite produces an alloy of iron and chromium

Most chromium metal is used to make stainless steel. This shiny steel is used to make things that must not get rusty, such as cutlery.

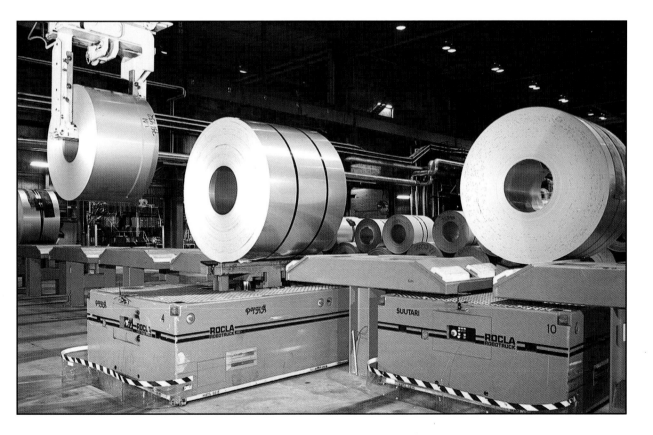

ATOMS AT WORK

During smelting, the solid chromite is heated by burning the coke until the chromite melts.

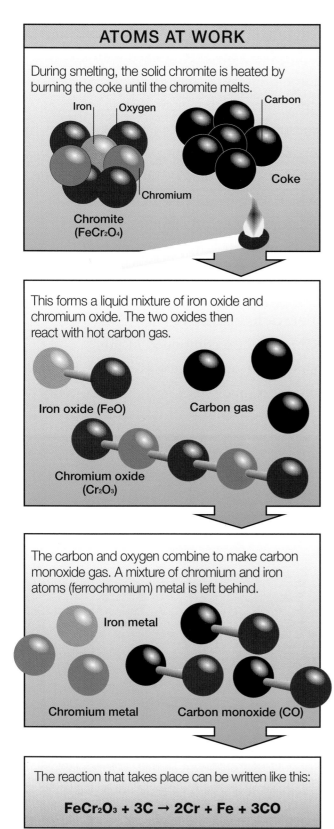

Chromite
$(FeCr_2O_4)$

This forms a liquid mixture of iron oxide and chromium oxide. The two oxides then react with hot carbon gas.

Iron oxide (FeO)

Carbon gas

Chromium oxide
(Cr_2O_3)

The carbon and oxygen combine to make carbon monoxide gas. A mixture of chromium and iron atoms (ferrochromium) metal is left behind.

Iron metal

Chromium metal   Carbon monoxide (CO)

The reaction that takes place can be written like this:

$$FeCr_2O_3 + 3C \rightarrow 2Cr + Fe + 3CO$$

called ferrochromium. (Alloys are mixtures of metals. Steel, for example, is an alloy of iron, carbon, and other elements.)

Inside the smelter, the carbon in the coke reacts with the oxygen in the chromite, leaving behind ferrochromium alloy. This reaction takes place above 3600 °F (2000 °C). The carbon atoms pull the oxygens from chromium atoms to make carbon monoxide (CO) gas. This gas then begins to burn making the smelter hotter and causing the smelting to go even faster.

Ferrochromium is more useful than pure chromium. Stainless steel, which is used to make cutlery and sinks, is made using iron and chromium. Therefore, the ferrochromium mixture already contains the main ingredients needed for such items.

DID YOU KNOW?

DRESSING THE ORE

Before chromite ore is refined using chemical methods, it is purified using physical techniques. This process is called dressing. First the ore is crushed up into a powder. In some cases magnets are used to remove any particles of chromite in the powder. (Chromite contains iron, which is attracted to magnets.) Any waste left behind, called gangue, is thrown away. Other refineries mix the crushed ore with water and bubble air through it. The chromite clings to the bubbles and rises to the surface, and the gangue sinks to the bottom. The chromite is then collected and refined by smelting.

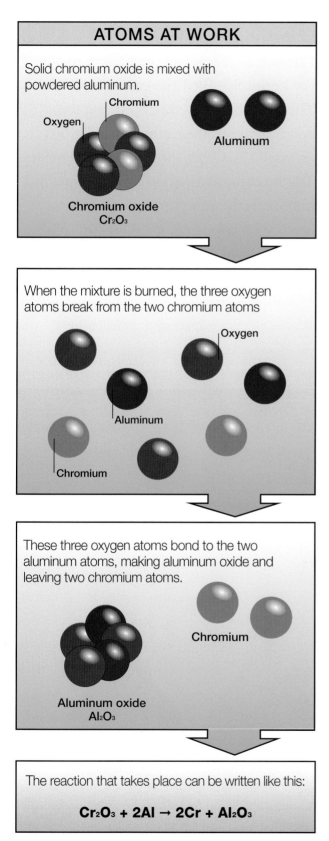

ATOMS AT WORK

Solid chromium oxide is mixed with powdered aluminum.

Chromium

Oxygen

Aluminum

Chromium oxide
Cr_2O_3

When the mixture is burned, the three oxygen atoms break from the two chromium atoms

Oxygen

Aluminum

Chromium

These three oxygen atoms bond to the two aluminum atoms, making aluminum oxide and leaving two chromium atoms.

Chromium

Aluminum oxide
Al_2O_3

The reaction that takes place can be written like this:

$$Cr_2O_3 + 2Al \rightarrow 2Cr + Al_2O_3$$

Pure chromium

Refineries can produce pure chromium. However, this is more difficult than making ferrochromium because the chromium atoms have to be separated from the iron atoms.

First the iron in the ferrochromium is replaced with sodium to make sodium chromate (Na_2CrO_4). This is then made into chromium oxide (Cr_2O_3). The oxide is mixed with powdered aluminum and set on fire. This creates a powerful burning reaction, which produces a lot of heat. The powdered aluminum burns at more than 3,600 °F (2,000 °C). At this temperature the oxygen atoms in chromium oxide bind to aluminum rather than chromium. The hot chromium is left as a liquid with waste aluminum oxide floating on top.

Chemistry and compounds

Like all elements, chromium combines with other substances to make compounds. These are structures of atoms held together by chemical bonds. Chemistry is the study of the way that elements and their compounds combine and react. Chromium compounds have many uses. The colorful ones are used in paints. Others are very corrosive and are used as cleaning agents.

Chromium oxides

Chromium reacts with oxygen to make hard crystals called chromium oxides. These are held together by strong ionic bonds between their atoms (see the box on page 17). Other metals also form oxides. The most familiar oxide is rust, a type of iron oxide. Rusting happens when iron reacts with oxygen in air. Rust can weaken,

Chromium compounds are brightly colored. Chromium chloride is pale violet, chromium nitrate is green, potassium chromate is yellow, while potassium dichromate is orange.

or corrode, a piece of iron. Chromium is less reactive than iron, and it does not corrode when it is exposed to air.

The most stable oxide of chromium is a green solid called chromium (III) oxide. It has the chemical formula Cr_2O_3. When oxygen bonds to a metal, each oxygen atom takes two electrons from the metal atoms to make a negatively charged O^{2-} ion. A chromium (III) ion is produced when a chromium atom loses three electrons to become a positively charged Cr^{3+} ion. (III is "3" in Roman numbers). Three oxygen ions and two chromium (III) ions combine into an uncharged molecule called chromium oxide. This has the chemical formula Cr_2O_3.

DID YOU KNOW?

CHEMICAL BONDS
Chemical bonds hold atoms together in complex shapes. There are two main types of bonds.
Ionic bonds: One atom gives outer electrons to another atom. Because electrons are negatively charged, the atom losing electrons gets a positive charge. The atom gaining electrons gets a negative charge. The atoms become positive and negative ions. Opposite charges attract, so these ions bond together. Ionic bonds are usually between metals and nonmetals.
Covalent bonds: Two atoms share some of their outer electrons. The shared electrons are attracted to each atom's positively charged nucleus, keeping the atoms together.

This bowl of orange ammonium dichromate is being heated. The heat is breaking up the dichromate into chromic oxide and nitrogen gas. The heat and gas produced by the reaction causes flakes of oxide to fly into the air. This is nicknamed the "volcano effect."

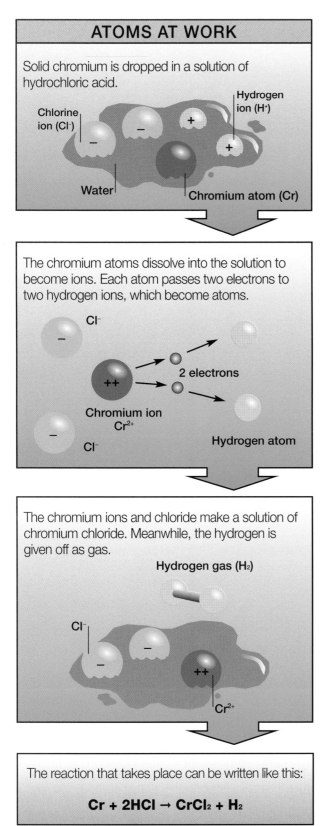

ATOMS AT WORK

Solid chromium is dropped in a solution of hydrochloric acid.

Chlorine ion (Cl⁻)

Hydrogen ion (H⁺)

Water

Chromium atom (Cr)

The chromium atoms dissolve into the solution to become ions. Each atom passes two electrons to two hydrogen ions, which become atoms.

Cl⁻

++

Chromium ion
Cr^{2+}

2 electrons

Cl⁻

Hydrogen atom

The chromium ions and chloride make a solution of chromium chloride. Meanwhile, the hydrogen is given off as gas.

Hydrogen gas (H₂)

Cl⁻

++

Cr^{2+}

The reaction that takes place can be written like this:

$$Cr + 2HCl \rightarrow CrCl_2 + H_2$$

Another oxide of chromium forms reactive, red crystals called chromium (VI) oxide (CrO_3). In this compound, the chromium (VI) ion (Cr^{6+}) has lost six electrons. (VI is "6" in Roman numbers).

The ways that atoms lose electrons to make ions are called their oxidation states. Chromium has three oxidation states: chromium (III), chromium (VI), and chromium (II), which it forms when it reacts with certain chemicals.

Chromium in acid

When pure chromium is dropped in acid, the metal fizzes as the corrosive acid reacts with it. This fizzing is caused by bubbles of hydrogen gas (H_2) being released. (If this gas is collected in an upside-down test tube and then lit with a flame, it produces a high-pitched pop.)

All acids contain hydrogen ions (H^+) dissolved in water. For example, hydrochloric acid (HCl) contains hydrogen ions with chloride ions (Cl^-)—made when chlorine atoms gains an extra electron. This acid reacts with chromium by making chromium (II) ions. At the same time two hydrogen atoms bond into a hydrogen (H_2) gas molecule.

If the acid and chromium react fully no hydrogen is left behind. The water then contains just chromium and chloride ions. Boiling off the water leaves white crystals of chromium (II) chloride ($CrCl_2$).

Chromates and dichromates

Chromate compounds contain one chromium and four oxygen atoms. Together these form a complex chromate ion $[CrO_4]^{2-}$. The four oxygen atoms in a chromate ion each need to share two electrons with the chromium atom. However, the most electrons a chromium atom can share is six, so the chromate ion takes two electrons from another atom. This gives the complex its 2- charge. In lead chromate ($PbCrO_4$) the two extra electrons come from a lead atom. The lead then becomes a Pb^{2+} ion. Lead chromate is a very widely used chromate. It is more commonly known as chrome yellow.

Lead chromate ($PbCrO_4$) crystals are bright yellow. This compound is also known as chrome yellow. Potassium dichromate ($K_2Cr_2O_7$) crystals are darker. Both compounds are used to color paints.

Dichromate chemicals contain two chromium and seven oxygen atoms which form a $[Cr_2O_7]^{2-}$ ion. They are used in the red chemical potassium dichromate ($K_2Cr_2O_7$). This substance is used to make dyes, photographic film, and fireworks. A mixture sulfuric acid (H_2SO_4) and sodium dichromate ($Na_2Cr_2O_7$) is used to clean glass. The mixture reacts with any dirt on the glass, but it also causes nasty burns if it comes in contact with the skin.

Uses of chromium metal

Some types of stainless steel, such as those used to make these pipes, contain tungsten and nickel atoms as well as chromium. This makes them very strong.

Chromium metal is used mainly as an ingredient in mixtures of other metals. A mixture of metals is called an alloy. Alloys behave differently from pure metals, often combining the best features of each ingredient. Stainless steel is the most common alloy to contain chromium. Another common use of chromium is as a shiny chrome coating which protects metal objects from rusting.

Stainless steel

This strong, shiny metal is found everywhere in modern life. It is used to make a variety of things from a surgeon's scalpels (cutting tools) to a skyscraper's reinforcements. Since the early 1900s stainless steel has been a marvel of technology because it never rusts. Before stainless steel, metal objects often rusted. Today stainless instruments are tough and long-lasting.

All types of steel are a mixture of iron and other metals with a little carbon. The carbon makes the iron harder and less likely to shatter. Steel is an extremely tough, durable alloy with many uses. However, the iron in regular steel rusts when exposed to air, which both looks bad and weakens the material. Stainless steel solves this problem by containing between 10 and 20 percent chromium mixed into the iron and carbon in the

DID YOU KNOW?

WHY STAINLESS STEEL IS STAINLESS
Stainless steel contains atoms of iron, chromium, and a few other elements. Iron would normally react with oxygen in air to make rust, or iron (III) oxide (Fe_2O_3). However, the chromium in stainless steel reacts with the oxygen instead to make chromium (III) oxide (Cr_2O_3). This compound forms an invisible layer over the steel that stops air from reaching the iron. The steel does not tarnish (change color), making it stainless.

steel. This makes the alloy tough and resistant to corrosion, which makes it stay clean and strong for a long time.

Chrome plating

Most people see pure chromium as a shiny covering on the fenders of old-fashioned automobiles and motorcycles. This thin layer of chromium is both decorative and protects against damage or corrosion.

Chemical engineers cover objects in chrome by a process called electroplating. A metal object is placed in a liquid with Cr^{6+} ions dissolved in it. An electric current is passed through the liquid to coat the object with chromium metal. Electricity comes in the form of a stream of electrons,

These car parts have been electroplated in an acid bath of chromium ions. The coating not only looks good, but it will protect the metal underneath.

which flows through the metal object into the chromium solution and then out from the solution through another terminal, or electrode. The electrons combine with the Cr^{6+} ions to make uncharged chromium atoms. These atoms stick to the metal object, forming a layer of chromium.

Chromium electroplating is a dangerous process. An easy way to release Cr^{6+} ions is by dissolving chromium (VI) oxide in acid. However, such strong acid solutions are very corrosive and the chromium (VI) ions are poisonous.

Chromium carbide (Cr_3C_2) is another hard coating for metals. Its main use is as a wear-resistant covering on engine parts. This compound of chromium and carbon is applied with a spray or by arc welding.

DID YOU KNOW?

RUBY-COATED ALUMINUM

Aluminum is made resistant to corrosion in a process called anodizing. The surface of the metal is treated with oxygen. This forms a protective coating of aluminum oxide (Al_2O_3), which is also found as the mineral corundum. Often the anodizing is done in a tank of chromium oxide (Cr_2O_3) solution, which leaves a small amount of chromium in the oxide coating. The dark red gemstone ruby is corundum with a small amount of chromium in it. The anodized surface of the aluminum is actually ruby, although it is far too thin to look red. The metal used to cover buildings and satellites is anodized to make it very tough.

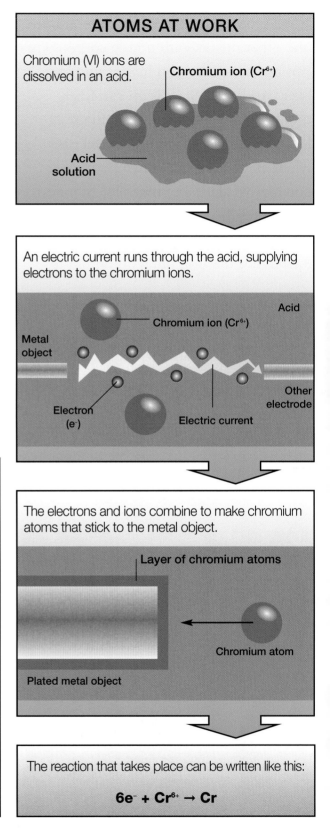

ATOMS AT WORK

Chromium (VI) ions are dissolved in an acid.

Chromium ion (Cr^{6+})

Acid solution

An electric current runs through the acid, supplying electrons to the chromium ions.

Acid

Chromium ion (Cr^{6+})

Metal object

Electron (e^-)

Electric current

Other electrode

The electrons and ions combine to make chromium atoms that stick to the metal object.

Layer of chromium atoms

Chromium atom

Plated metal object

The reaction that takes place can be written like this:

$$6e^- + Cr^{6+} \rightarrow Cr$$

Chromium and fabrics

Chromium compounds are used to prepare clothing for everyday wear. They make fabrics soft and supple and are also used in the dyeing process.

Tanning is the process that turns animal skins into leather. The skins are dipped in chemicals that make them durable but also softer and more pliable. Various substances are good for tanning. In the past, Native American people used the fats and brains of animals to make a soft leather called buckskin. Today, factories use vegetable and chrome tanning. Vegetable tanning uses chemicals from tree bark, while chrome tanning uses dichromate chemicals. Chrome tanning typically takes a day, while vegetable tanning takes several weeks.

Colored chromates

The other main use of chromium compounds is for dyeing fabrics. These chemicals make a color stick to cloth. The colors stay bright after washing and do not stain the skin. Chrome dyes were very popular in the nineteenth and early twentieth centuries. However, the waste they produce is poisonous, so other dyes are now more common.

Tanned animal skin is removed from giant drums after being treated with dichromates at a tannery— a leather-producing plant.

Colorful chromium

The element chromium was named for the Greek word for color because its compounds are brightly colored. These substances make good ingredients in paints and dyes. Chromium also gives some precious gemstones their color.

One of the most widely used chromium pigments is chrome yellow, or lead chromate ($PbCrO_4$). This is ground into a fine powder and dissolved in an oily liquid, such as turpentine, to make a paint. Chrome paints were widely used until the 1980s. At that time people became concerned that the lead in the paints was a health hazard. Since then alternative pigments have been developed. Another chromium pigment is chromium oxide green, or chromium (III) oxide (Cr_2O_3). Soldiers use it to paint camouflage on their faces.

A green chromium-containing powder sinks to the bottom of a test tube. This compound does not dissolve in water and is used in oil-based paints.

CHROMIUM FACTS	
COLORS OF CHROMIUM COMPOUNDS	
⬤ chromium (II) fluoride (CrF_2)	green
⬤ chromium (II) chloride ($CrCl_2$)	white
⬤ chromium (III) oxide (Cr_2O_3)	green
⬤ chromium (VI) oxide (CrO_3)	deep red
⬤ lead (II) chromate ($PbCrO_4$)	yellow
⬤ silver (I) chromate (Ag_2CrO_4)	brown
⬤ potassium dichromate ($K_2Cr_2O_7$)	red

Without chromium ions inside their crystals, rubies would not have their vibrant red color.

Gemstones

Emeralds and rubies take their vivid green or red colors from small amounts of chromium. Without the chromium both gemstones would be clear and completely colorless crystals.

Ruby is based on a crystal of aluminum (III) oxide (Al_2O_2), also known as the mineral corundum. Pure corundum is see-through and has no color. It is the hardest known substance after diamond. Corundum's structure is a repeating arrangement of aluminum and oxygen ions. Replacing about one in every hundred aluminum ions with a chromium ion colors the crystal red, which is then called ruby.

Emerald is based on beryl crystals. Beryl has the long chemical formula $Be_3Al_2(SiO_3)_6$. Beryl crystals also form a regular lattice of beryllium, aluminum, and silicate (SiO_3) ions. Swapping some aluminum ions with chromium ions makes the crystal green.

DID YOU KNOW?
THE DIFFERENCE BETWEEN RUBIES AND SAPPHIRES Both rubies and sapphires are crystals of the same corundum mineral. Completely pure corundum is a clear crystal of aluminum oxide (Al_2O_3). However, tiny amounts of impurities give the crystals their bright colors. Chromium impurities make them red to make rubies. Cobalt impurities color the crystals blue to make sapphires.

Chromium and life

Chromium is unusual because a person needs one type of compound in his or her diet, but another type of chromium compound is a deadly poison. Food has the healthy chromium (III) form. Many factory chemicals contain the poisonous chromium (VI). When this second group of compounds is released in industrial waste it damages the environment.

Diet

Many foods contain healthy chromium (III), including grains, potatoes, and broccoli. Black pepper is also very high in chromium but is usually eaten in small amounts. Because reports say chromium (III) helps dieting and reducing cholesterol, some people take it as a health-food supplement. Doctors are even investigating whether it helps diabetics, who cannot easily use the sugar in their blood for powering their bodies.

Scientists believe that chromium plays an important role for turning blood sugar into energy. After a meal there are high levels of sugar in the blood. The body responds by releasing insulin from an organ called the pancreas. This chemical

Peppercorns have a large amount of healthy chromium (III) ions in them.

tells the body tissues to absorb the sugar and store it or use it. Chromium is thought to help the body respond to insulin. For example, people eating too little chromium have difficulty absorbing blood sugar.

The amount of chromium needed in food is very small. Most people need just a millionth of an ounce (28 µg) a day.

Environmental problems

Only the chromium (VI) form is dangerous to living things. Chemical compounds with chromium (VI) ions are found in industrial chemicals that are used in some paints and for tanning leather. These compounds include lead chromate and potassium dichromate.

Chromium (VI) is very toxic. Breathing it in can cause asthma or nosebleeds. It can also cause a nasty rash on the skin. Chromium (VI) compounds can even kill

Diabetics must inject themselves with insulin to control the sugar in their blood. Scientists believe chromium (III) ions help the body use insulin.

a person. If it is released as waste into rivers or buried underground, chromium (VI) can poison wildlife. Some old industrial wastelands still have dangerous amounts of chromium in their soil.

CHROMIUM FACTS

FOODS CONTAINING CHROMIUM

Many foods contain a large percentage of an adult's daily chromium needs.

● Broccoli—½ cup	37%
● Processed turkey—3 ounces (85 g)	35%
● Grape juice—8 fluid ounces (237 ml)	25%
● Waffle	22%
● Potatoes—1 cup	9%
● Orange juice—8 fluid ounces (237 ml)	7%
● Beef—3 ounces (85 g)	7%
● Banana	3%

Periodic table

Everything in the universe is made from combinations of substances called elements. Elements are made of tiny particles called atoms, which are too small to see.

The character of an atom depends on how many even tinier particles called protons there are in its center, or nucleus. An element's atomic number is the same as the number of protons.

Scientists have found around 116 different elements. About 90 elements occur naturally on Earth. The rest have been made in experiments.

All these elements are set out on a chart called the periodic table. This lists all the elements in order according to their atomic number.

The elements at the left of the table are metals. Those at the right are nonmetals. Between the metals and the nonmetals are the metalloids, which sometimes act like metals and sometimes like nonmetals.

● On the left of the table are the alkali metals. These have just one outer electron.

● Metals get more reactive as you go down a group. The most reactive nonmetals are at the top of the table.

● On the right of the periodic table are the noble gases. These elements have full outer shells.

● The number of electrons orbiting the nucleus increases down each group.

● Elements in the same group have the same number of electrons in their outer shells.

● The transition metals are in the middle of the table, between Groups II and III.

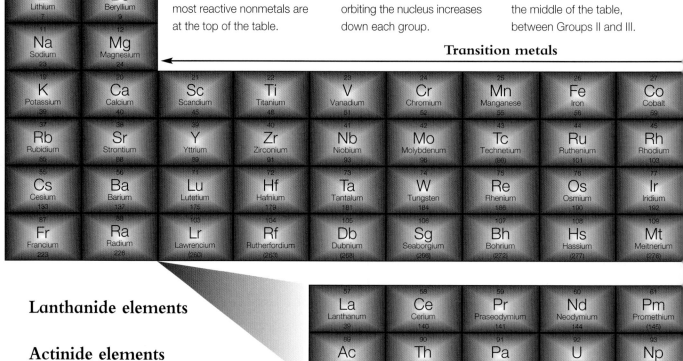

Group I

Group II

Transition metals

| 1 H Hydrogen 1 | | | | | | | | |

3 Li Lithium 7	4 Be Beryllium 9							
11 Na Sodium 23	12 Mg Magnesium 24							
19 K Potassium 39	20 Ca Calcium 40	21 Sc Scandium 45	22 Ti Titanium 48	23 V Vanadium 51	24 Cr Chromium 52	25 Mn Manganese 55	26 Fe Iron 56	27 Co Cobalt 59
37 Rb Rubidium 85	38 Sr Strontium 88	39 Y Yttrium 89	40 Zr Zirconium 91	41 Nb Niobium 93	42 Mo Molybdenum 96	43 Tc Technetium (98)	44 Ru Ruthenium 101	45 Rh Rhodium 103
55 Cs Cesium 133	56 Ba Barium 137	71 Lu Lutetium 175	72 Hf Hafnium 179	73 Ta Tantalum 181	74 W Tungsten 184	75 Re Rhenium 186	76 Os Osmium 190	77 Ir Iridium 192
87 Fr Francium 223	88 Ra Radium 226	103 Lr Lawrencium (260)	104 Rf Rutherfordium (263)	105 Db Dubnium (268)	106 Sg Seaborgium (266)	107 Bh Bohrium (272)	108 Hs Hassium (277)	109 Mt Meitnerium (276)

Lanthanide elements

Actinide elements

| 57 La Lanthanum 39 | 58 Ce Cerium 140 | 59 Pr Praseodymium 141 | 60 Nd Neodymium 144 | 61 Pm Promethium (145) |
| 89 Ac Actinium 227 | 90 Th Thorium 232 | 91 Pa Protactinium 231 | 92 U Uranium 238 | 93 Np Neptunium (237) |

The horizontal rows are called periods. As you go across a period, the atomic number increases by one from each element to the next. The vertical columns are called groups. Elements get heavier as you go down a group. All the elements in a group have the same number of electrons in their outer shells. This means they react in similar ways.

The transition metals fall between Groups II and III. Their electron shells fill up in an unusual way. The lanthanide elements and the actinide elements are set apart from the main table to make it easier to read. All the lanthanide elements and the actinide elements are quite rare.

Chromium in the table

Chromium is in the first period of the transition metals. Like other transition metals, chromium atoms have empty spaces in both their two outermost electron shells. This allows them to form large complicated ions, which can have a variety of charges. Chromium compounds have several colors, such as yellow and red.

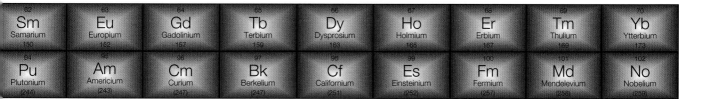

Key:
- Metals
- Metalloids (semimetals)
- Nonmetals

24 / Cr / Chromium / 52
- 24 — Atomic (proton) number
- Cr — Symbol
- Chromium — Name
- 52 — Atomic mass

Group VIII

Group III	Group IV	Group V	Group VI	Group VII	Group VIII
					2 He Helium 4
5 B Boron 11	6 C Carbon 12	7 N Nitrogen 14	8 O Oxygen 16	9 F Fluorine 19	10 Ne Neon 20
13 Al Aluminum 27	14 Si Silicon 28	15 P Phosphorus 31	16 S Sulfur 32	17 Cl Chlorine 35	18 Ar Argon 40

28 Ni Nickel 59	29 Cu Copper 64	30 Zn Zinc 65	31 Ga Gallium 70	32 Ge Germanium 73	33 As Arsenic 75	34 Se Selenium 79	35 Br Bromine 80	36 Kr Krypton 84
46 Pd Palladium 106	47 Ag Silver 108	48 Cd Cadmium 112	49 In Indium 115	50 Sn Tin 119	51 Sb Antimony 122	52 Te Tellurium 128	53 I Iodine 127	54 Xe Xenon 131
78 Pt Platinum 195	79 Au Gold 197	80 Hg Mercury 201	81 Tl Thallium 204	82 Pb Lead 207	83 Bi Bismuth 209	84 Po Polonium (209)	85 At Astatine (210)	86 Rn Radon (222)
110 Ds Darmstadtium (281)	111 Rg Roentgenium (280)	112 Uub Ununbium (285)	113 Uut Ununtrium (284)	114 Uuq Ununquadium (289)	115 Uup Ununpentium (288)	116 Uuh Ununhexium (292)		

62 Sm Samarium 150	63 Eu Europium 152	64 Gd Gadolinium 157	65 Tb Terbium 159	66 Dy Dysprosium 163	67 Ho Holmium 165	68 Er Erbium 167	69 Tm Thulium 169	70 Yb Ytterbium 173
94 Pu Plutonium (244)	95 Am Americium (243)	96 Cm Curium (247)	97 Bk Berkelium (247)	98 Cf Californium (251)	99 Es Einsteinium (252)	100 Fm Fermium (257)	101 Md Mendelevium (258)	102 No Nobelium (259)

Chemical reactions

Chemical reactions are going on all the time. Some reactions involve just two substances; others many more. But whenever a reaction takes place, at least one substance is changed.

In a chemical reaction, the atoms stay the same. But they join up in different combinations to form new molecules.

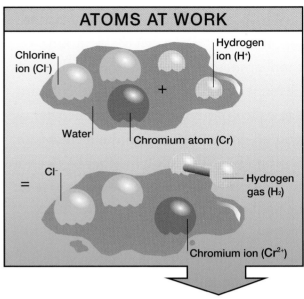

ATOMS AT WORK

Chlorine ion (Cl⁻)

Hydrogen ion (H⁺)

+

Water

Chromium atom (Cr)

= Cl⁻

Hydrogen gas (H₂)

Chromium ion (Cr²⁺)

The reaction that takes place when chromium reacts with hydrochloric acid is written like this:

Cr + 2HCl → CrCl₂ + H₂

This tells us that one atom of chromium reacts with two molecules of hydrochloric acid to give one dissolved molecule of chromium dichloride and one molecule of hydrogen gas.

Chromium hydroxide is produced when sodium hydroxide is added to a solution of chromium ions. Chromium hydroxide does not dissolve and it settles to the bottom as gray-green powder.

Writing an equation

Chemical reactions can be described by writing down the arrangements of the atoms involved before and after the reaction. The number of atoms before will be the same as the number of atoms after. Chemists write the reaction as an equation.

When the numbers of each atom on both sides of the equation are equal, the equation is balanced. If the numbers are not equal, something is wrong. So the chemist adjusts the number of atoms involved until the equation does balance.

Glossary

acid: An acid is a chemical that releases hydrogen ions easily during reactions.

atom: The smallest part of an element having all the properties of that element. Each atom is less than a millionth of an inch in diameter.

atomic mass number: The number of protons and neutrons in an atom.

atomic number: The number of protons in the nucleus of an atom.

bond: The attraction between two atoms, or ions, that holds them together.

compound: A new substance made when two or more elements chemically join together.

corrosion: The eating away of a material by reaction with other chemicals, often oxygen and moisture in the air.

crystal: A solid consisting of a repeating pattern of atoms, ions, or molecules.

electrode: A material that exchanges electrons with another electrode.

electron: A tiny particle with a negative charge. Electrons are found inside atoms, where they move around the nucleus in layers called electron shells.

electroplating: A process that uses an electric current through a solution of metal ions to coat a object with a metal.

element: A substance that is made from only one type of atom.

equation: An expression using numbers and symbols to explain how a chemical reaction takes place.

gangue: The unwanted material mixed in with an ore or other useful mineral.

ion: An atom or a group of atoms that has lost or gained electrons to become electrically charged.

metal: An element on the left-hand side of the periodic table.

mineral: A compound or element as it is found in its natural form in Earth.

neutron: A tiny particle with no electrical charge. Neutrons are found in the nucleus of almost every atom.

nucleus: The dense structure at the center of an atom. Protons and neutrons are found inside the nucleus of an atom.

periodic table: A chart of all the chemical elements laid out in order of their atomic number.

proton: A tiny particle with a positive charge. Protons are found inside the nucleus of an atom.

reaction: A process in which two or more elements or compounds combine to produce new substances.

solution: A liquid that has another substance dissolved in it.

transition metal: An element positioned in the middle of the periodic table. Transition metals, including chromium, have spaces in their outer electron shell and in the next shell in.

Index